MAN‖‖‖‖‖‖‖‖‖‖‖‖‖‖‖SS

T0078411

INSPIRED LIFE: MANTRAS FOR SUCCESS

PROF. B.S. AHLUWALIA

PARTRIDGE
A Penguin Company

Copyright © 2013, 2015 by Prof. B.S. Ahluwalia.

ISBN:	Hardcover	978-1-4828-1086-8
	Softcover	978-1-4828-1087-5
	Ebook	978-1-4828-1085-1

All rights reserved. No part of this book may be used or reproduced by any means, graphic, electronic, or mechanical, including photocopying, recording, taping or by any information storage retrieval system without the written permission of the publisher except in the case of brief quotations embodied in critical articles and reviews.

Because of the dynamic nature of the Internet, any web addresses or links contained in this book may have changed since publication and may no longer be valid. The views expressed in this work are solely those of the author and do not necessarily reflect the views of the publisher, and the publisher hereby disclaims any responsibility for them.

To order additional copies of this book, contact
Partridge India
000 800 10062 62
orders.india@partridgepublishing.com

www.partridgepublishing.com/india

The universe is infinite but our
perceptions are finite,
Our dreams are infinite but
our vision is finite,
Our potential is infinite but
our efforts are finite,
Our opportunities are infinite but
our capabilities are finite.
Our greed is infinite though
our needs are finite,
He is infinite but our faith
and prayers are finite,
Though love is infinite, thankfully
our hatred is finite.

—*Prof B.S. Ahluwalia*

DEDICATED TO

My spiritual parents Sh. R.M. Singh Kandal, an Engineer from Formen Christian College and Smt.Chander Kanta, a graduate from Fateh Chand college, who inculcated rich ethical and social values in me that have always been my source of inspiration.

ACKNOWLEDGEMENTS

I am thankful to my wife, **Sunita Ahluwalia** and my children for their unstinted support and encouragement.

CONTENTS

ABOUT THE AUTHOR

Professor B.S. Ahluwalia is a visiting faculty of a number of Management Institutes in Delhi, specializing in Human Relations and Operations Management.

He has retired as Chief General Manager, Ministry of Defence (Navy), which he had joined through Engineering Services.

During his stint with MOD (Navy) and after retirement, he has extensively travelled in countries like Sweden, UK, Germany, Israel, South Africa, France, Australia and Malaysia.

He also had the opportunity to learn about the values and different cultures of Southern and Western India during his postings at various stations, while serving the MOD.

After taking voluntary retirement, he developed interest in academics, astrology and writing. He is a graduate Mechanical Engineer from DCE and M.B.A from FMS Delhi. He is life member and Fellow of All India Management Association (FIMA).

PREFACE

Success is the most sought after thing in every person's life- whether it is succeeding in professional life, business or relationship. And the interesting thing about success is that it can be achieved in different ways. One can succeed in business or profession by being ethical or by cheating, frauds etc. In our day to day life we come across various instances of cheating and frauds. The end result is same, which is, getting rich and achieving your goals, but therein lays the BIG difference. When a person leads principled, ethical and honest life, he may take longer to succeed but his success will be longer lasting and he will be at peace with himself. On the other hand the person who achieves success through cheating and shot cuts may achieve quick results but his success will be short lived and he will be always under stress. In this book when we talk of success we mean success based on principles and ethics. The sole purpose of this book is discuss and find ways and means of achieving true, long term success.

For achieving true success in any area we need three things i.e. knowledge, skills, and character. For character we need to have principles, ethics and rich values. It therefore becomes necessary to understand the fundamentals about principles, ethics, traditions and values which are close to our heart. This can be understood only when we learn and practice spirituality. For this purpose the first few chapters of this book are on spirituality.

Nature has given us two very powerful entities namely Mind and Body. Our mind is so powerful that we can conceive great ideas and grandiose designs for us, to achieve. Our Mind works round the clock. Similarly our Body, which is the visible part, is the most sophisticated and powerful machine capable of achieving anything that our mind decides.

The most important part is that with help of these entities we can do, both good and bad things. It is for us to decide whether we do negative things or positive things. To ensure that we use our Mind and Body for doing only good and positive things it is necessary that we get necessary training and guidance. To achieve this objective we need to practice spirituality.

There are already large number of books and publications on spirituality but their language, content and philosophy is put across in very sophisticated way. Most of the people, particularly youngsters, stop reading these books because they find them very complicated and are unable to relate and identify with the subject. Whereas, spirituality is very personal and important for each one of us. Some of the writers express their philosophy in such a complicated way that it appears that their objective is to show their knowledge on the subject rather than communicate with the reader. The difficult language and philosophy scares away and discourages common man and thereby prevent him from getting the real benefits of spirituality.

This book has been written to help readers understand the philosophy of spirituality in a simple manner. The objective is to explain the power of spirituality in such a way that even common man can understand and he is therefore encouraged to practice spirituality on day to day basis and thereby derive tangible benefits. To achieve this objective, effort has been made to help everybody to relate with the subject. Although this book has been written in Indian context, the content and the spirit is valid for all, across physical borders.

These days, increasing competition and growing aspirations are causing a lot of stress and therefore, spirituality has become all the more important to overcome such stress.

Nature has blessed us with three most powerful things in the form of our Body, Mind and Soul. As you read along you will realize the self-curing powers of our body and the power of faith in achieving our desired goals and even healing. One important thing to understand is that spirituality is a very powerful regime not only in building our personality but it can also act as a course corrector. This happens when in our hectic schedules and urge to prosper in a short span of time, we lose track of what is right and what is wrong. Spirituality brings about a sense of discipline and total wellbeing in us. Whatever we do, be it yoga, prayers (puja). listening to discourses, fasting or seeking blessings of any Deity, it is we and only we only who are going to be benefited. We therefore do all these activities and ceremonies for ourselves. In no way do these affect anybody else including the Deity we worship. We do such things voluntarily.

Some astrologer or pundit may recommend these ceremonies but the net objective is our welfare. Even when we give alms to a beggar it benefits us, that is why we give. The beggar gets benefited in the bargain. So it is win-win situation for both. That is why it is one of the most common things that we all do. Even giving donations, charity and doing social work, without any personal motive, benefits us.

Power of giving is sublime if it is used without any ulterior motive. Only the fortunate get this power. It is also one of the best ways to improve our self-esteem, which is very important for all of us. So when we give money or donate anything to the needy, priest or a religious Institution, don't think we are doing a favor. We are doing it because we want to do it. You find many corporate leaders contributing to charity. They want to give and share their prosperity with the needy. This is central philosophy of this book.

If we follow spiritual path it will be we and only we who will be benefited physically, materially, intellectually and emotionally.

Spirituality and Religion.

Religion is an organized collection of beliefs, values and faith, which we respect and cherish and therefore propagate and spread these through preaching and discourses, for the welfare of Humanity. Religion gives its followers an identity. The binding force of religion is so strong that its followers are even ready to die for it.

Why So Many Religions?

The reasons for this are geographical, variations in values, customs and ego of the preachers. All religions preach almost similar things. But over the years, because of ego problems of the preachers, difference of opinions, oppression by the ruling class or circumstances or combination of these, new religions have evolved. For example, Sikhism has born out of circumstances.

The ego of Preachers is evident from the fact that almost all important religions have been split into various sects. We have Roman Catholics, Protestants and Anglicans in Christianity although Christ is same. Shias and Sunnis in Islam, Namdhari, Amitdhari and Nirankari and many more in Sikhs, Jainis also have four major sects and in Hinduism there are a large number of sects. So much so that even worshippers of Krishna are divided into two, namely one which recites Radhey-Krishna and the other recites Radhey-Radhey.

If one looks at the core of different religions and sects, the preaching and values are quite similar with minor changes here and there. Let us look at the sacred words i.e. Aum (OM), Ameen and Amen. Just see the extent of similarity in them and all these are very sacred for the respective religions namely Hinduism, Islam and Christianity respectively.

One can be spiritual without
being religious.
But one cannot be religious
without being spiritual.

Prof. B.S. Ahluwalia

HOW TO READ
THIS BOOK

The initial chapters are to prepare the back ground so as to facilitate understand the philosophy of the book. Don't get disillusioned, continue reading. As you go along, the content will become more meaningful.

This book is not a one-time read. While reading this book, you may find certain things which may be contrary to your views and ideas. Actually when you will read it for the first time you may be able to relate with the subject to the extent of only 60%.

Subsequent readings may help you to relate with subject to about 80%. There after you will find yourself thinking about spiritual issues closer to your heart. When this happens it will mean that the book is now making you move along the spiritual path, on your own. It will be very important mile stone in your move towards spirituality. This will mean a new beginning for you and that is the objective of this book.

Still you should continue to read this book, once a week or fortnight or whenever you feel like. This will ensure that you continue to move along the spiritual path which you have chosen. Otherwise, in the busy day to day schedule you may lose track. Yes, there is no need to read the whole book, time and again. Read any chapter which you may like to read at that particular moment. This is therefore, a bed side book.

Prof. B.S. Ahluwalia

Know the self to be sitting
in the chariot,
the body to be the chariot,
the intellect the character,
and mind the reins.

—*Upanishad*

1. SPIRITUALITY FOR BEGINNERS

When we look at ourselves we find that we are made of broadly three components namely Body, Mind and Soul. One of them i.e. Body, is visible and the other two components are invisible.

Our Body is the hardware which is visible and it gives us our identity therefore we give lot of importance to our looks. The invisible parts are Mind and Soul which are more crucial for our well-being but we don't pay similar attention to them.

Our Soul is the guiding force like a guru/mentor which provides only guidance. It is indestructible and is independent of our body. So when we die, soul moves out and enters body of another living thing. When soul enters any Body, the life begins and when soul leaves any Body, death occurs. Soul is not the 'doer' or Karta. It only guides us like a mentor.

Mind on the other hand is the 'Pilot' driving our Body. Nothing happens without the command from our Mind. Mind is the 'doer' or the 'Karta' of our Being. Mind plans and executes its 'Will' through various parts of our body. It's the mind which decides what we do, good or bad. Our mind acts through our brain which is the Super Computer. Though invisible, mind is the CEO our body. When we die the mind also dies.

We are made of 5 basic elements (pancha tatva) namely earth, water, fire, air and ether.

Our physical body, the solid mass is made of earth. Our body is the densest form of energy in solid state. Maintaining body in good condition ensures healthy body, self-confidence and sense of security. It is the body which gives us our identity.

The water element is evident from the fact that it constitutes more than 70% or our body. The water element also represents vitality, sexuality and emotions.

The fire element is in the form of energy and represents ego, temper/anger and self-righteousness.

The air element is associated with love, sincerity, compassion and spirituality.

The ether element represents pure consciousness, wisdom, self-realization and is part of the soul.

What is Spirituality?

Spirituality is the food for our mind and soul. It helps to enrich our knowledge about rituals, traditions, values, beliefs and customs so that we understand their importance and effectively use the power of our mind and soul. Spirituality is universal, it is not specific to any caste, creed or religion nor is there any specific age to practice spirituality. Spirituality provides you the framework for purer thoughts and actions.

Spirituality is a journey— Spirituality is process of transforming one's self to achieve a healthy Body, a calm Mind and sound relationship with our Soul and Environment. Spirituality is not about religion but about individual, his thoughts, values, beliefs and faith. No one says that Christianity is spiritual.

What we say is that so and so is a very spiritual person.

Since we normally don't go for any formal education in the field of spirituality, to go along the road of spirituality, we need a guide/ mentor. It is here that religion has a very useful role to play. We can get guidance through a Guru/mentor or religion or both. The sole aim is—Integration of Body, Mind and Soul—attaining **ONENESS**.

All of us can't achieve complete integration of Body, Mind and Soul because that is the ultimate level, but we can certainly move in that direction. For example, many of us take to Engineering and Medicine as their careers. Although every one aspires to reach the top but only few reach that level. Most of us achieve excellence in their fields but to some extent. Same is true if we practice spirituality, each one of us can reach some level of spirituality through our thoughts and deeds. The more spiritual we are, purer will be our thoughts and more noble will be our deeds. That's why those who achieve complete synchronization of Body, Mind and Soul are called noble people and are often referred to as Saints and spiritual Gurus. Such people are very few and far between.

By healthy body we mean that we eat Satvik food, lead active life so that all the sub systems of our body remain fit and healthy.

By calm Mind we mean that we are able to control our thoughts and actions. It is very difficult to control our Mind. All our good and bad thoughts and actions are creation of our mind. When we are able to control our Mind, we are in a better position to decide what is good and what is bad and our decisions are more in sync with the inner voice of our Soul. Our long term aim should be to have complete control over Mind. This can only be achieved through Abhyasa (practice) Yoga. As we go along this process, we achieve certain level of control over our Mind. That's why Spirituality is a journey.

Sound relationship with our environment means that our relations with the society and people around us are good and healthy. We take care of our environment including plants, trees, rivers, animals and birds etc. who are part and parcel of our system.

It is good to have an end to
the journey forward,
But it is the journey that
matters in the end.

Earnest Hemmingway

Why Spirituality?

There are two dimensions of the need for spirituality. One external and the other is internal. We all know that soul is indestructible and after death it moves from one living thing to another, not necessarily, human. When it moves from one body to another, there may be major or minor change of physical and social environment. Whatever be the case, there is need for the soul to get adjusted to the new environment by way of faith, traditions, values and beliefs. This adjustment of the soul to the new environment can only be achieved through spirituality.

Only a well-adjusted soul can guide the new Being smoothly through its new life. Therefore spirituality is essential to achieve this integration of the Soul with the environment. This is the external dimension of need for spirituality.

At individual level, as we go through the life, the ups and downs are part of life. We feel stressed at times due to relationship problems, health problems, financial problems, or sudden loss of dear ones etc. We often face situations where one feels lost or helpless. It is during such times that spirituality acts like an anchor. It provides emotional support at the time of crisis. It helps individual to see things in a better perspective and therefore helps him to successfully face the day to day problems. During difficult times, it is the faith in yourself and your Guru/God, which carries you through the troubled waters. It is this internal dimension of spirituality which comes to your rescue.

The other aspect at individual level is the need to keep a balance in life. All of us want to be rich and powerful. The strange part is that most of the people can't absorb money and power. The moment they become rich or powerful, it goes to their head. They become arrogant and ruthless. It therefore results in their downfall. The higher the level from which they fall, more the hurt it causes. We can find so many examples around us. It is here that spirituality can play a very useful. When one becomes powerful, spirituality is not only helpful, but it acts as a force multiplier. Because spirituality not only helps us to control our ego but also stabilizes our mind; it leads to better and balanced decision making. When we get rich or become powerful, spirituality helps in keeping negative propensities, like ego, greed, lust and anger at bay. We can spread the power of spirituality through our actions and encourage our co-employees to practice spirituality as well. One of the best ways to practice spirituality in management is to include it in the 'Mission Statement'. You should frame your policies in such a way that employees who are competent, sincere and hardworking get rewarded. Sycophancy and favoritism should be discouraged at all levels. Reward integrity. The work environment should be such that the employees experience only healthy stress. There should be balance between the official and personal life. Some organizations turn blind eye to the personal responsibilities of their employees. This leads to stress and this has direct bearing on their performance. Off-late a number of organizations are realizing this aspect and have modified their policies to bring about balance between personal and official life.

For a society/ race, spirituality is as important as for an individual. For any society to be strong and prosperous, it is essential to have strong beliefs, ethics, values, tolerance and sense of discipline. If you look back into history, you will find that everybody remembers societies/ races which had these traits, with respect and awe. Whenever any society, race or country has been found deficient in spirituality, it has led to violence, wars and destruction. Sometimes when the rulers move away from the spiritual path, their negativities take charge of their mind thereby causing oppression and misery to their people. When this happens, it leads to revolutions. History is full of such instances. Another thing is that if there is deficiency in spirituality in any society, its members are not capable of maintaining emotional balance when they are under stress or when faced with problems. They break down and therefore face emotional and physical problems. They have no anchor to hold on, when in trouble or they have no Guru to whom they can look up to, for guidance and help, when needed. It is therefore very important for any society/ race to be spiritual.

Spirituality makes people better human beings.

I visited Israel in the year 2001. Since Israel is militarily very strong and has been fighting wars for last few decades, I had a very different image of people of Israel. I thought that they will be warrior like and trigger happy. But what I found was that Israeli people are very spiritual. This is one of their important assets which have been helping them pull through the

crisis. It is not easy for any
small country to survive when
surrounded by adversaries. But
Israeli people have not only
survived but have been 'Winners'.
They are fighting war of survival
and being spiritual at the same
time.

I observed another very
interesting thing in Israel.
During discussions at lunch
time, one individual asked the
location of a small village in
India. I had no idea and then he
mentioned Kangra. I said yes, I
know Kangra. He told me that this
village is near the place where
Dalai Lama is living. Then I told
him about Dharamshala and asked
him as to how he is talking about
a village near Dharamshala. He
told me that his son has gone to
that village for holidaying. I
was really surprised as to why
any youngster from Israel should
go all the way to such a remote

village for a holiday. Then he explained in detail.

In Israel, all youngsters, after completing their school are drafted to serve in Defence Forces for 2 years. During these two years they save enough money. After completing their 2 year's tenure, all children invariably go on holiday for one year. The idea is to see and explore the distant places of their interest. Most of them including girls, normally, go alone and to distant remote places to get real experience of life. After coming back they pursue their further studies.

Just imagine the amount of personality development they undergo in just 3 years. Two years of disciplined life in Defence followed by one year of exploration of the world and the self, at the same time. It forms the solid foundation for strong character and personality.

Our scientific knowledge
has outrun our
Spiritual knowledge,
That is why we have guided missiles
and misguided leaders/men

Martin Luther King Jr.

Spirituality for Whom

There are quite a few misconceptions about spirituality. Some people think that spirituality is about religion. Some think that spirituality is only for senior citizens. Others think that being spiritual means being old fashioned. All views are based on insufficient knowledge, incorrect perceptions, wrong notions and not so good experiences about spirituality.

The problem has been compounded by fake gurus and so called greedy god-men. The fact is that all of us practice spirituality right from childhood through various moral and religious stories, epics and biographies of great people. As a child we visit shrines with our parents with all respect and fervor.

When we start growing we start getting into the worldly things and therefore get distracted from spirituality. We feel that it is difficult to meet your growing material demands as well as practice spirituality. We perceive that there is conflict between spirituality and our day to day life style. The fact is that spirituality is for all. It is a journey, a long journey. The ultimate goal is to achieve self-realization and enlightenment but very few reach this level. This should not discourage us. All of us can practice spirituality without compromising our worldly duties.

Actually spirituality is very helpful in meeting our worldly demands because it takes one towards a healthy body and a calm mind. While moving through the life, every one faces ups and downs. If you practices spirituality regularly you will face minimal 'downs' and achieve maximum growth. Also at the time of crises, spirituality helps you in overcoming the hardships in a much better way. You will find that spirituality brings about positive changes in your life, thinking and makes life more meaningful. Further, practicing spirituality is not at all time consuming. You don't need long hours, even a few minutes, on regular basis, are enough to give you a healthy body and a calm mind. For best results make spirituality as part of your life style.

Spirituality and You

Spirituality is part and parcel of all of us. Some of us realise it, others practice spirituality unknowingly. One reason for this is that we are introduced to spirituality at a very young age. It happens even before our formal education begins and this is done by our

parents and close relatives.
Spirituality is the foundation
on which we develop and build
our physical, intellectual and
emotional being. It is like roots
of a tree called life, our life.
It is essential that we take
care of our foundation. It needs
constant attention, nurturing
and strengthening so as to make
our life healthy and prosperous.

As we grow, we get exposed to
the good and bad habits, thoughts
and actions. Our net personality
depends on the strengths of
good and bad qualities. If
good qualities outweigh bad
qualities we become spiritually
good person. If bad qualities
outweigh good qualities we become
spiritually deficient person.
Even the cruelest of kings and
hard core criminals have some
goodness but this goodness gets
overshadowed by the negative
propensities and results in
the bad deeds done by such

people. Under such circumstances spirituality provides the best way forward.

Spirituality helps in bringing about the goodness of the person to the fore and helps the person chose the right path and thereby guides him to arrive at better decisions. Even for common people, spirituality is the best way to overcome their negative traits, and have peace of mind, which ultimately leads to stress free and healthy body. If there is no spirituality, there is nothing to prevent human beings from becoming cruel, selfish and violent. When this happens it leads to destruction of the race/society.

Therefore spirituality is essential for any race/society to flourish and progress.

Be not afraid of taking a small step,
Be afraid of standing still.

—Chinese Proverb

Action Plan I

- ➢ Remember, spirituality is a journey.
- ➢ Use spirituality as a course corrector.
- ➢ You don't have to neglect your worldly duties to practice spirituality. It should be all inclusive.
- ➢ There is no age restriction for practicing spirituality, it is for everyone. Once you are convinced, practice spirituality in your day to day life.
- ➢ Realize the power of spirituality. Put it in use, and get full benefits of spirituality.
- ➢ Spirituality will ensure that you have a healthy body and calm mind so that your thoughts and actions become wealth creators.

2. OUR BODY—THE SUPER MACHINE

Our body is the most wonderful machine in the world. It's a world in itself, full of large varieties of millions of living things. Each part of our body is a piece of technological excellence. Since it is part of all of us we don't look at it as closely as we should. We just take it for granted. The perfection with which each part and sub—system has been designed is amazing.

Does anyone know the age as to when he is going to die? No, because our body is a perfect work of engineering. It is capable of growing, rejuvenating and self-curing/healing. If we properly look after our body and lead stress free life we can go on living far beyond 100 years. Technically our life is limitless because there is no limit laid down. Then how do we decide the life span? It is just statistics and varies from region to region and country to country. This variation is due to various factors like our food habits, stress levels, health and attention we pay to our body. At present, if we ignore deaths by accidents, then average age spans between 60 and 90 years. Just imagine, there is variation of 50% on the average, which is huge by any standard. And with increasing awareness the upper range will go on increasing.

Just imagine, according to one statistics in China, no individual under the age of 64 has ever died of heart attack. We have read in scriptures that in olden days life span used to be in hundreds of years. Now scientists are already working to increase the age span in a big way. This is possible because of the capabilities of our body.

Look at the capabilities of our brain. No super computer is anywhere near the capabilities of our brain. Similarly we have Heart, Kidneys, Liver and host of other organs which work round the clock, carrying out very complicated processes, without creating any noise or pollution. We can call our body a 'wonder machine'. It is limitless. It is we who draw lines and restrict its use to a small fraction vis—a-vis its capabilities.

Couple of decades ago the fastest man used to take 15

seconds to cover 100 meters. Today it has reached sub 10 seconds level. During every Olympic Games new records are made, higher achievements are attained. No limits are laid down. It is the contestants who lay down the limits.

All of us are capable of reaching that level in sports but just see how just a few of us reach that level. This is not true only in sports; it is true in every field of life. It is we who lay down limits and draw boundaries, otherwise our potential & capabilities are limitless.

Our Brain is not only a super computer it is much more than a computer. It has life. The capabilities of a normal computer are constrained by its configuration. If your requirements exceed your computer's capabilities, you have no choice but to buy a new computer or upgrade your RAM or Hard Disk. There are no such constraints in case of our brain. It has no limits. Our brain keeps on developing. It is we who draw the limits and restrict our brain's capabilities.

Once we decide to learn anything, our mind helps our brain to upgrade. What is needed is determination and commitment. The fact of the matter is that we use only a small fraction of our brain.

Unfortunately we humans have tendency to limit our growth and this fact gets ingrained in each one of us, right from our childhood. Our parents decide as to what level we should grow. For some people graduation is a big target. For others it could be becoming a doctor or an engineer.

Once that target is achieved we stop growing. Such targets are in turn governed by our needs and aspirations. Even in case of spiritual gurus, once they reach a certain level in terms of spirituality, following and financial stability, they stop growing. Then they get distracted to the materialistic and worldly propensities, thereby stunting their further spiritual growth. Their mind and brain gets re-tuned to the new direction. Their actions become more commercial than spiritual.

All of us have same brain and capabilities, to start with, but just see the scale of variation as far as our achievements are concerned. The fact of life is that we are not aware of capabilities of our brain and its potential and therefore we never set higher targets.

Now let us look at our muscles. All our physical activities, including the pumping of blood by our heart, is done by our muscles. These include walking, running, weight lifting etc. We can't do any physical activity without using our muscles. The working and capabilities of our muscles are great and amazing.

The best part is that through practice we can improve the power of our muscles and hence their capabilities. Unlike the machines developed by we human beings, movement of muscles do not generate heat, noise or produce pollution.

We don't realize, but observe the working and performance of our heart. It goes on pumping blood 24x7, without any break.

Now let us analyze our mouth .We use it for talking and eating. If we can control our mouth we can avoid most of our problems, may be all our problems arising out of poor eating and rash/ lose talk. All our relationship problems arise out of lose/ negative talk.

We are masters of the
words not spoken
But, slave of words spoken

—*Chinese Proverb*

Every spoken word is like firing a bullet from the gun. Once it is out it can't be put back. If we can have control on what we say and think before opening our mouth we won't have any relationship problems. This will in turn reduce stress to a great extent and therefore give us peace of mind and a healthy body.

Similarly if we have control over our eating habits, we can avoid most of the food related diseases including the problems related to over eating.

Now let us have a look inside the mouth. Our teeth help us in chewing the food. While chewing, our gums discharge the wonderful thing called saliva. Saliva has all the chemicals that help us digest our food. Saliva has another great property—it also acts like cleaning agent of our teeth. So as we eat our food our teeth also get cleaned. Thus the more we chew our food better will be our digestion and cleaner will be our teeth. Brushing our teeth assists in cleaning our teeth. Brushing removes plaque and any food particles that get struck between teeth. The saliva which gets produced during brushing also helps in cleaning the teeth. To produce more saliva, the tooth paste manufacturers and sugar and salt.

To keep your gums healthy we can give them exercise by eating sugar free chewing gum. In olden days we used to clean our teeth with small wooden sticks called 'Dattun'. These were taken from Neem and Kikker trees. The procedure was that first you chew one end till it becomes soft and then brush your teeth with this soft end. What actually was happening that while chewing the datun, our gums were getting exercise and were also producing saliva at the same time. And, finally we cleaned our teeth with softened wood with the saliva acting as the cleaning agent. The Neem tree sticks though bitter, were still better because they had additional antibacterial properties. Another way to have healthy teeth and gums is to use electric tooth brush. The vibrating bristles clean the teeth very effectively and also give good massage the gums. For best results use small round head. If you use electric brush even thrice a week, you can avoid visits to the dentists.

All the taste which we enjoy while eating is felt through the taste buds located on our tongue. The color of your tongue gives the clear indication of condition of our digestive system. Clean and pink tongue indicates healthy digestion. When we go to doctor, examination of the tongue is one of the first things done by the doctor.

Therefore, if we pay due attention to what we speak, what we eat and how we eat, we can avoid most of our problems, physical and emotional, avoid stress and therefore have peace of mind, a very important step towards a successful life.

The Healing Power of Our Body

A word of caution. While highlighting the curing powers of our Mind & Body, the idea is not to belittle the role and achievements of doctors and medical science. They have very important role when we fall sick or have any medical problems.

You will be surprised to know that our body has a strong inbuilt immune system which is capable of fighting all diseases and has curative powers.

Over a period of time and due to neglect of our body by us, our immune system becomes weak. It is is one of the reasons that we take help of medicines. In case of most of the day to day diseases the medicines normally play only limited active role in curing our disease. They mostly play passive role and help and assist our body to cure itself.

In case of fractures, it is healing system of our body which joins the bones. The orthopedic surgeon aligns the bones and 'sets' them and puts plaster to prevent movement of the fractured bone. It does not heal or join the bones. Plaster only helps by preventing any movement. The bones get joined by the healing system of our body.

As regards the medicines prescribed by the doctor, in this case, they are basically pain killers so that we get relief from pain. These pain killers play no role in joining of the fractured bones. It is our body mechanism which is joining the broken bones.

It is commonly known that it takes 72 hrs. to cure common cold with medicines and it will take 3 days to cure on its own.

In case of jaundice, chickenpox, viral infection etc. it is our body which cures them. Doctor gives medicines to keep the body temperature under control and advises food restrictions so as to accelerate the recovery. These things play a passive role in actually curing the diseases. Sometimes, when we are sick Doctors prescribe some medicines to strengthen our immune system to enable quicker recovery.

Yes, doctor makes our recovery faster and plays a very important role of a faith healer as well. The very talk and touch of doctor does wonder because the patient has faith in the doctor.

Our mind plays very important role and helps our body to recover from any disease. It is our mind which provides strength to our immune system and faith in the doctor. Without positive participation of our mind, our body cannot fight any disease.

The idea here is not to undermine the role of the doctors or the medicines but to highlight the powers our mind and body, about which most of us are ignorant.

You must have observed that a number of medicines are sold under their generic names as well as under brand names. The cost of branded medicines is many times more than the generic medicines although clinically they are same.

If you treat two patients, having identical problems, one with generic medicine and the other with branded medicine, and if both the patients are informed about this fact, then you will observe faster recovery in case of patient who has been given branded medicine. If you don't tell them anything then in that case the recovery will be identical.

Patients always have more faith in doctor who prescribes costlier medicines, although they may feel the financial pinch. People don't like to go to a doctor who prescribes cheaper and only white tablets. People get cured faster with colorful and expensive medicines although they have no special formulations. It's all in the Mind.

If you have faith, anybody
can heel you.
Be it a doctor,
Your guru,
Your god,
Godman or even a soothsayer.

Prof. B.S.Ahluwalia

You may not be aware but a large number of diseases are caused by stress. These include common cold, asthma, heart diseases, depression, headaches, acidity, hypertension type 2 diabetes etc. The other important cause of some diseases could be lack of physical exercise, our life style, Tamasik food and polluted environment. In some cases, diseases are of hereditary nature. This means that the problem is inherent in our genes.

Thus you will see that most of the time the diseases are mind related (Stress) or body related (malfunctioning of organs) and both these things can be controlled through spirituality. If we practice spirituality, we can avoid most of the diseases.

In addition to the physical diseases and hurts, in our day to day life, we experience emotional hurts. These could be due to harsh words spoken by someone or when someone hurts your feelings. Such problems, though not physically visible cause much more serious medical problems than sickness. Sometimes we are not even aware of such mind related problems/ stress. These could manifest in the form of common cold, headaches, asthma, hypertension etc. If left unattended, such problems can last for years and could have serious consequences by way of weakening of our immune system, damage our organs and thereby leading to serious health problems.

Spirituality provides the best way forward in combating such problems. It is high time that the modern Medicine recognizes the power of our Body and Mind in curing/healing and integrate it in their treatments. It will lead to amazing results in fighting various diseases including Cancer. Meditation is one of the best ways to overcome such stress related problems..

The other option could be seeking help of your Guru or Mentor. Spirituality also preaches forgiveness which result in reducing stress and this also is one of the ways to overcome such emotional problems caused by hurt.

What is the importance of Vaccination of small children: When the baby is very small, its immune system is not strong enough to fight the infections present in the environment, to which it gets exposed. In order to strengthen its immune system it therefore becomes essential to provide external help through a series of vaccinations/ injections to provide wide area of protection. Actually we are only strengthening their body's immune system to enable it fight the infections to which they are likely to be exposed as they grow.

Our Body-Potential

Every human being has the potential for greatness
—Bo Bennett

God has given same machine /body to every one of us. The capabilities of our body are both, amazing and mind boggling. Is it not strange as to how little we make use of the power of our body?

It is just like our Cell Phones. When we buy any Cell Phone, we go for the one, having maximum number features and applications. Actually we don't even use 10 % of the features. In fact most of us are not even aware of more than 50 % of the features of our Cell Phones. As regards the remaining 40% of the features we don't know how to use them. Despite all this, we pay for all the features, most of which remain redundant and we never use them. But we are always eager to show and tell others about the power of our cell phone and feel proud to display it.

It the same way we treat our body. We look after the external exposed parts of our body and are proud to display it but actually we are using at the best, only 30% of the capabilities of our body.

We are capable of doing wonders but we waste our time and energy by idling or doing negative things or useless things, guided by ego, greed and jealousy.

Don't treat your body like a cell phone. Realize the potential of your body and start exploiting your capabilities. Get going by having dreams and ambitions. No dream is too big for your Body. Make use of your Brain by learning new things and update your professional knowledge to achieve excellence in your profession. Eat healthy (Satvik) food. Keep yourself fit through physical exercise (Yoga) to ensure that all your organs like Heart, Kidney, Liver etc. are in good shape.

For achieving anything worthwhile, a fit and healthy Body is a must. Inculcate this habit in children so that they follow disciplined daily routine. But in real life all of us are very careless and casual and take our body for granted. Our life styles are getting very laid back. The Fast Food culture has further complicated this issue because of its adverse effect on our health. Remember, we are what we eat.

Our ancestors and Gurus have however made provisions to overcome the side effects of such bad habits and ensure that we lead healthy lifestyle. They have devised the ritual of Fasting. Fasts give break to our laid back food habits. They bring into

focus the need to look at our
eating habits and also a sense
of self discipline to control
our senses. To ensure that we
undertake such fasts seriously,
they have given them religious
color. This brings about a sense
of importance and fear of the
unknown.

Actually when we undertake
Fasts, it is we who are benefited.
Fasts help us in disciplining
our mind and to control our
senses. These fasts are for our
well-being. In no way they have
any effect on the Deity in whose
name we keep fast. Muslims keep
Roza for 40 days every year. It
is considered one of the toughest
/rituals. But such strict rituals
bring about a sense of discipline
for both mind and senses of the
body. This is one of the best
rituals and strongest features
of Islam. Even Christians keep
fast during 40 days preceding
Easter.

Action Plan II

➢ Realize the potential of your body.

➢ Keep your body in good shape through exercise and yoga, to exploit its full potential.

➢ The more you use your body, including organs like brain, muscles and heart, healthier will they be and better will be their performance.

➢ Give purer inputs of food, air and water to your body.

3. MIND—THE CEO

Man Is But Product of His Thoughts

—Mahatma Gandhi

Mind is the most active part of our Being. Actually it is super active and has wildly roaming tendencies. Our mind does not remain still at any time. In split second it moves from one area of interest to another. One of the main objectives of spirituality is to learn as to how to control our mind. Since mind is CEO of our body it is very essential that we have a calm mind. For meeting the goals and objectives of our life we need to be focused and should have ability to concentrate on our tasks. This is possible only if we have control over our mind. Towards this end we must make effort and train and develop our mind. The quality of our actions is direct reflection of state of our Mind. As we grow, our mind develops. As a child the development of the mind is through informal training and reflex actions. Our immediate social environment and our mother are the first trainers of our Mind.

Our formal training starts when we start going to school. As we go along with formal training we still continue with the informal training through our social environment and relationships.

As we grow, our mind develops and slowly it acquires the ability to take decisions. The quality of our decisions is directly proportional to the quality of training that our mind has undergone. As we grow, we pick up good habits, have our dreams and ambitions. Along with this we also pick up bad habits like gambling, drinking, lying and negative propensities, like greed, jealousy, ego etc.

We are what our thoughts are—Thoughts are the seeds for any action that we take. Therefore for our actions to be right it is important that our thoughts are right. By right thoughts I mean, we should have positive thoughts, for a worthy action, without any prejudice and bias. When our thoughts are positive good actions and worthy goals are achieved, and we are at peace with ourselves. If our thoughts are negative, prejudiced and

malicious, so will our actions be.
Such actions bring about stress
and negativity in our life. Once
we take this road, it is very
difficult to change. It becomes
a vicious circle and therefore
our mind remains disturbed at all
times. Over a period of time it
becomes a habit and we fail to
realize the cause of disturbed
mind and stress.

We are what our deeds are—We
are known by our name but are
remembered for our deeds, good
or bad. Therefore it is important
that our deeds are not only good
but noble as well.

Another important thing is,
whether our deeds are only for
ourselves or they are for benefit
of others as well. When we work
for ourselves, we fulfill our
desires and needs and therefore
it benefits us. But real happiness
comes when we look around us and
do something for others. It could
be helping a needy, planting and

nurturing trees or feeding birds and animals because they are part of the system in which we live. They are connected to us in some way or other. When we help somebody without any personal gain or motive, it is service to humanity. You try and you will find that it will not only give you satisfaction but also improves your self-esteem. If you have low esteem then this is one of the best ways to improve your self-esteem.

We are what we eat—Nature has given us a wonderful thing called Body. For growth and maintenance of our body we need air and food. The quality of these inputs has direct impact on us. If we eat Satvic (fresh, less spicy) food, it keeps us not only healthy but helps in keeping our mind calm. Rajasika (spicy, non veg.) food on the other hand, may be tastier but makes us aggressive, thereby making our mind restless. We should therefore eat less spicy, fresh and balanced food.

We are what company we keep— The effect of company varies according to the stage of life, the individual is. As a child the friends have great influence on the personality development of the child. Those children who lack company or detest company are likely to grow as loners. Those boys who happen to have more girls as company, may land up with split personality. Similarly a girl child having mostly boys as friends will have a tom boy personality. It is therefore important for parents to make sure that their child gets not only the right company but a right blend of company.

The most important stage to have good company is when boys are between 17 to 20 years and girls 13 to 18 years. It is at this stage that they are most vulnerable. Most of the bad habits get picked up at this stage. Children tend to choose careers more on advice of their friends than parents. This is also the stage when the so called generation gap is at its peak. It is therefore important that parents keep an eye on the company of their children, be proactive and provide them guidance.

As one becomes an adult, the nature of company changes. The company now becomes more transient and fast changing. One meets new colleagues, moves on to new places, increases his social circle. One can't have close relationship with all. It is therefore important to choose and nurture close relationships only with whom one shares common interests and values.

As one starts growing professionally, and heads for the top slot, one starts getting feeling of loneliness. This is because it is lonely at the top.

At this stage the type of company one keeps is crucial, both, personally and professionally. It is difficult to decide as to who is sincere and who is closer to you to take advantage of your position. Any wrong company at this stage can prove very expensive Both, personally and professionally. One should therefore try to have company of matured people of character, having good vision and values. One should avoid 'yes men' and sycophants. Many Companies have gone bankrupt because the top executive lacked good company and was surrounded by people of low integrity and poor vision.

It is not always possible to choose your company and in practical life it becomes difficult to know who is good and who is bad. To overcome this problem, spirituality provides the best option. If you are spiritual, the chances of your going wrong get minimized. Spirituality will help you control your ego, stabilize your mind and keep you away from the negativities like, ego, greed, anger, conceit etc. Your actions will be more in tune with your soul. You will automatically move towards the people of good character and vision.

Desires

We all have desires. Our desires are a great motivating factor in achieving our goals. That's why it is often said that to achieve any big goal one should have a burning desire.

Yes, having desires is a good thing but they need to be moderated and controlled through sublimation. Uncontrolled desires lead to violent and animal like behavior. Some spiritual gurus suggest that we should not have desires. Some go to the extent of saying that if we give up all our desires, we will reach the ultimate level of spirituality and ultimate bliss. In my personal opinion, I don't think it is correct.

Nobody can lead healthy and happy life without having any desires. One has to have desires to lead meaningful life. It could be desire to excel or desire to even attain nirvana. Even if you want to renounce your all desires and achieve ultimate bliss, you have to have a desire to achieve this goal. You can't achieve anything without working for it and for this you have to have desire.

Any person who has no desires left in life will start degenerating, physically, emotionally and mentally. You must have observed that when any patient is not recovering from any sickness, people start saying that he has lost desire to live or he has no will to live.

Controlled desires are the essence of life that keeps us motivated. Desires are good. It is greed which is destructive.

When I was young, in my teens, I had a crush on a girl. I would stand in my courtyard at a particular time, waiting for her to come back from school. One day while I was standing in the court yard, my mother came and just said 'You must deserve before you desire.' These words had great impact on me.

My mother had great way of conveying very important things. She used to be very firm and to the point. This is how I learnt the basic rule about desires, which is that, we must become worthy of our desires to get full benefits of our efforts.

Our thoughts are seeds
for our actions,
Our actions are seeds for our deeds,
Our deeds are seeds for our habits,
Our habits are seeds
for our character.

—Anonymous

Negativities of Our Mind

The negativities are urges, negative habits and emotions like ego, greed, jealousy, lust, conceit, fear, anger etc.

We all have ego problems and are jealous when the other person is happy. This is happening because we don't focus on real issues and our mind is not able to concentrate in the right direction.

Most of the time our mind moves towards negative propensities such as, ego, greed and jealousy. We get sadistic pleasure out of criticizing and hurting others. I will give you a practical example.

As you know, all the Bosses have the 'powers to give' benefits or to deny you benefits. They can exercise their powers in both ways. You will be surprised to know that most of the bosses show their powers by denial. They get sadistic pleasure by denying you the benefits. They don't realize that 'power to give' is sublime. 'Power to give' is far more superior and satisfying than power of denial. Still very few Bosses exercise their 'powers to give'. Perhaps they also had Bosses who practiced 'power to deny'.

Our ego, jealousy and anger encourage us to harm others. It is very strange but true that we feel bad if somebody has been rewarded, promoted, has a nice house, rich in-laws or has achieved some land mark. It may not have any effect on us but we feel disturbed out of sheer jealousy. Some people even go to the extent of cursing those who are prospering. This particularly true of office colleagues and close relatives even, brothers, sisters, their spouses, cousins etc.

Another strange aspect is that people try to compete with their near and dear ones.

I don't know why people have tendency to compete with their close relatives and friends when there is whole world out there to compete with. By doing so they are limiting their goals and dreams. They are just lowering their limits. This tendency also generates negative tendencies like jealousy, greed and stress.

Another strange thing about us is that if we are told some adverse thing about some person, we immediately believe him. For example if somebody tells you that so and so is corrupt or having an affair, we immediately believe him.

Sometimes we even go to the extent of reinforcing his claim by saying that I always suspected it. We never try to find the truth and take such statements for granted. We get some sort of sadistic pleasure when we hear such things.

On the other hand if somebody tells us that so and so is an honest person or has very strong character, we take it with a pinch of salt. At every occasion we will try to verify this statement. The moment we find that he has done something wrong, it gives us pleasure and we feel happy that we have proved that he is not honest.

The reason for this behavior is that we feel happy when we find that somebody is worse than us and feel unhappy to know that somebody is better than us, although he has nothing to do with us. By doing this we are only wasting our time and energy.

We tie ourselves with negative habits
And then complain that
life is very difficult.

—*Anonymous*

Reflecting Back

Just try this experiment for a few days—Before going to bed at night, reflect back on the things you have done during the day. How many good deeds you have done, anything professionally constructive , bad things like hurting someone, told lies or abused anybody.

You will realize that most of the time has been wasted on petty things and hardly anything worthwhile has been done. Despite this, we feel that we have been very busy and didn't have any time to even scratch our head. This is the reality with most of us.

Make it a habit, before going to bed, to reflect on the things you have done during the day. Think of both, good as well the negative things. Slowly you will find that you will be doing mostly good deeds.

This small action will not only bring peace of mind but help you to focus your mind in the positive direction.

Meditation

One of the best ways to control our mind is through controlling your thoughts. The way to control your thoughts is by Meditation. Some people also call it Concentration and some also call it Mind Stilling. The method and objective is same.

Meditation means sitting still, closing your eyes and concentrate your mind and controlling your thoughts. You can start meditating for 5 minutes and increase the time period to 10, 15, & 20 minutes.

Though Meditation appears very simple but in reality it is very difficult. You will observe that within few seconds your mind will start wandering. You will start thinking about your problems, relationships etc. The moment this happens, try to get back to Meditation. That is why Meditation requires lot of practice & dedication.

Don't get disheartened if you are not able to concentrate in the beginning. Have patience and persistence will help you. Actually if you can master the art of Meditation, more than half the battle is won. It means that you have learnt the art of controlling your mind and believe me it is a very big achievement.

When you meditate, you bring your mind closer to the soul. Your mind will follow the advice of soul and that means your deeds will be noble. That is the objective of spirituality.

Pranayama – The Powerful Yoga

Our Body is one of the greatest machines. It has its own mechanisms to react under different conditions. Whenever we are upset or feel disturbed, our breathing becomes irregular and faster. When we are at peace, our breathing is smoother and slower. Here the role of pranayama becomes important. One of the easiest ways to calm the mind is through Pranayama. Pranayama can be easily learnt from the trained Yoga teacher and can be mastered through practice.

Meditation through Pranayama is Transcendental Meditation (TM) propounded by Guru OSHO. In this one has to sit straight and concentrate on one's breathing. Thereby you achieve the twin objective of concentration and deep breathing, which is very healthy and blissful.

In addition to helping you in controlling your mind Pranayama has wonderful effect on your physical well-being.

Pranayama and Technology

For our survival, our body needs food, water and air. We can remain without food for a couple of weeks. We can remain without water for a couple of days but we cannot remain without air for more than a few minutes. This is because air is essential for working of our various organs including Brain. Air is essential for our survival whereas food and water help in sustaining life. That is why the yoga for inhailing air is called Pranayama, Prana means life. This yoga brings about feeling of tranquility and rejuvenation.

Another interesting thing of our body is that unlike other sub systems, nature has provided very small inlet and outlet for air. Actually our nose is used for both, inhaling as well as exhaling air and our nostrils automatically take turns to carry out these functions.

The amount of air which we inhale depends on the efficiency of our lungs which pump in and pump out air from our body. This process goes on automatically on 24x7 without our realizing it. The air which we inhale helps in purifying our blood and is essential for efficient functioning of our organs.

The more air we inhale better our health will be. To explain the importance of air intake, let me give you a practical example.

In this respect our cars also work on the same principal as our body. The amount of air intake has direct bearing on the performance of the car. If the air intake filter gets chocked, the supply of air to the car engine gets reduced and the efficiency of the engine goes down. If you want good millage from your car, one of the important things is to keep air filter clean.

If you still want to improve the performance of your car engine then your mechanic will advise you to either increase the size of the air intake pipe or recommend fitting of a turbocharger. That is why you will observe that cars fitted with turbochargers have much higher performance. Turbocharger is nothing but air compressor which increases the air supply to the engine. Pranayama acts like a turbocharger for our body.

We can increase the air supply to our body if we do Pranayama regularly. We can also increase the air supply through exercise because when we do any physical activity, our body seeks more air and therefore we start inhaling more air.

The end result is same, i.e. inhaling more air but there is difference between the two. In case of exercise, our breathing becomes faster but our air intake is not controlled but is triggered by increased demand of air by our body. In case of Pranayama the breathing is controlled and well regulated.

What is Holding You Back

The following behavior and habits come in the way of controlling our mind:

- We all know too much of anything is bad. Therefore, over indulgence in sleeping (laziness), talking, eating, drinking, or leading an immoral life.
- Interfering in someone else's affair and being critical.
- Be jealous of others.

- Being over-ambitious and therefore failing to achieve our goals.
- Carry guilt about a wrong doing.
- Our ego.
- Carry strong likes/ attachments, dislikes/ aversions, and self-righteousness.

Extreme Stress

Sorrow looks back, Worry looks around, And faith looks up.

—Anonymous

In real life one may have to face extreme stress due to serious disease, accident or death of near/dear one. Such situations result in extreme physical or emotional stress. To meet the challenge of such situations one should seek the refuge of Almighty.

At such times our behavior should be like a child. You will observe that whenever a child has fear or faces stressful situations, it rushes to the mother or father. The child has unflinching faith in his mother and father. The child seeks protection, shelter and reassurance from his guardian. The child just clutches them and refuses to leave till he is reassured.

Similarly we should remember Him and seek His help. This could be, by reciting His name and diverting your mind towards Him. What is important is that we have faith in Him. Faith is a great healer. Tough situations need tough responses to control your mind. The other option under the circumstances could be seeking help from your mentor or guru.

Action Plan III

➢ Eat satvik food.
➢ Be in the company of people having good values, vision and integrity.
➢ Develop habit of Positive thinking and noble thoughts.
➢ Give more than you get.
➢ Spend at least 10 minutes daily with yourself. Sit in a comfortable position, close your eyes and relax. Try to stabilize your mind
➢ Do Pranayama while Meditating. Practice TM
➢ Overcome your bad habits and negativities.
➢ Control your ego. Be respectful and humble.
➢ Never curse any person.
➢ If you achieve the ability to control your mind, you are bound to be a WINNER, both materially and spiritually.

4. SOUL—THE MENTOR

You are not human on a spiritual journey, You are a spirit on a human journey.
—Upanishad

Soul is independent of Mind and Body. It does not get affected by our environment or training. Spirituality is the food for soul. When the soul enters the Body, it may be coming from a different social, physical and religious environment In order to help the mind and soul to integrate with the present environment, it is essential to condition and acquaint the soul with the relevant values, customs and beliefs etc. Spirituality helps in integrating the soul, mind and body with the new environment.

Soul, although invisible, is the central part of our Being. It is the torch bearer of our life. Soul guides us to follow the path of truth without any ulterior motive. Whenever we think of doing any negative thing, our Soul cautions our mind. Our mind may follow the advice of soul or it may rationalize its action and go ahead with the original decision. Of course whatever our actions are, we have to bear the consequences of the same.

Most of the time when our mind goes against the wishes of our soul(inner voice) by rationalizing its actions, these decisions/actions are influenced by greed, jealousy, ego or short term gains. Naturally, the benefits will be short term but in the long run we will be losers. Also in the heart of heart we know that we have done wrong and therefore our mind remains restless/ disturbed.

During our life time we all get opportunities to prosper and fulfill our desires but quite often we all commit mistakes even blunders and lose these opportunities. But rather than accepting our mistakes, we start blaming others for our failures. Thus we refuse to learn from our mistakes. This happens when we don't listen to our inner voice i.e. our Soul, and rationalize our negative actions, which are influenced by ego, greed or jealousy.

To avoid such things what we need is a 'Guru' or mentor who would help us in taking right decisions at the right time.

The mentor can be our father, mother or any elder or our boss or any person whom we respect and hold in high esteem. Very few people chose Mentor or Guru because it is very difficult to decide and find a good mentor. The world is full of fake Gurus and Swamis. Therefore the most common alternate method adopted by most of us is to achieve this is through religion.

The other way is through Meditation, attending discourses delivered by Swamis and spiritual Gurus. Such discourses create an ambiance of peace and tranquility in our mind. Most of the discourses are about lives of great saints, epics, tales carrying moral lessons and their own experiences. They thus help us in reviewing our actions and thoughts and enhance our ability to choose between right and wrong.

When we have a Guru we bow to him. It brings out humility in us and therefore control one of the worst negative traits i.e. Ego. When we bow to our elders and Guru we also get blessed. Blessings are very important part of our life.

The only problem is that it is very difficult to identify a genuine Swami or Guru. Most of the self-proclaimed Swamis and dharam Gurus are fake and frauds, who are out to fleece and exploit their followers.

The alternate way to achieve this is that most of us follow the path of prayers. What is a prayer? Prayer is one way of connecting with your Guru/ God. Your Guru/God can not be present everywhere so you get connected through prayers. Prayers insulate you from you immediate social environment and encourage you to concentrate your mind towards your God. God can be anybody, of your choice, in whom you have unstinting faith. It is the faith which is the central thing in any prayer. Prayer is also one the ways of breaking away from your routine cores and spending time with 'yourself'. It makes you reflect on your deeds, both good and bad and helps you to choose the right path. It also helps you to connect your mind with your soul.

When we do our prayers it is we who are benefited. We are not doing any favor to the Deity being worshiped. Prayers help us in calming our mind and bring it in tune with our soul. It enhances our ability to decide between good and bad. It motivates us towards having purer thoughts and doing good deeds. After the prayers one feels refreshed and full of positive energy.

Power of Faith

Faith is one of the most powerful instruments with human beings and even other living things. Faith is part and parcel of each one of us. The degree of faith varies from individual to individual. Some of us are not aware of the fact that they have faith. Such people call themselves as rationalist. They look for logic in everything. Unfortunately it is their ego which is coming in the way of their acceptance of the fact that they have faith.

The simple fact of life is that you will not even go to a doctor unless you have faith in him. The other side of the coin is that no amount of medicine can cure you if you don't have faith in the medicine and the doctor.

Child has faith in his parents, we have faith in our Gurus and we all have faith in God.

If you don't have faith in yourself, it will affect your decision making capabilities and therefore your life. With the power of faith you can overcome most of your problems. Faith helps in reducing the intensity of hurt and pain and over a period of time, helps in overcoming our problems/ obstacles. That's why it is often said that Faith is a great healer.

One can have faith in Guru, or in any person for whom one has respect, scriptures, statues, photos, temples, animals, a ritual, or even a particular stone. The examples are, like having faith in Quran, statues of Gods, photographs of Gods/ Gurus, a particular church or temple, prayers and religious ceremonies or even some naturally shaped stone.

In India people even have faith in animals (Cows are worshiped), trees & plants (Peepal & Tulsi), rivers (Ganga) and fire and these form part of various rituals. What is most important is that one should have total unstinting faith, for faith to be effective. Faith is effective only when our devotion is complete and not superficial.

We can see and feel the power of faith in our day to day life. Small children have faith in their parents. When they fall sick, mere touching of their forehead or face by their mother or father brings immediate relief and smile on their face. They feel so safe, secure and loved that sometimes such actions even cure their sickness. This is the power of faith.

You can observe the opposite of this also. If the child is sick and the person (eg. mother) on whom he has faith is not around, no amount of medication will have any effect.

Adults experience similar results when they are sick. In their case, they have faith in the doctor who is treating them. You will observe that after the visit of the doctor, the patient feels much better even though no medicines have been given yet. This is because the patient has faith in that doctor. If the patient does not have faith in the doctor the patient's recovery will be slower.

Power of faith is so strong that in Hyderabad, during a particular period, one person has been feeding live fish to asthma patients and good percentage of patients feet that their asthma has been cured. Every year thousands of patients visit Hyderabad for this treatment. In reality it is their faith in that person and in the treatment which is treating them. Fish has no role in curing asthma, it is faith in the treatment which is providing them relief. If one does not have faith then he will not get cured. If it was not faith but the fish, which is curing the patients, then everybody can take fish, sitting at home, and get relief, without going to Hyderabad for this treatment.

There are so many instances like this and they are prevalent all over the world, in one form or the other.

What actually happens is that when we have faith our mind gets focused on the problem. When this happens, our mind activates our defence mechanisms, through increased immunity levels and we become more determined to fight the problem. Once our mind gets into action then it will stop at nothing short of complete success. That is why for faith to be effective it is essential to have full faith.

When we believe in God we also believe that He is everywhere. Still majority of us visit a particular shrine because we have faith in that shrine. It is this faith which is pulling millions of people to Mecca, Jerusalem, Varanasi, Golden Temple, Vaishnodevi, Tirupati, and Shirdi.

How Does Faith Work

Faith is one sided but has to be total. When we visit any shrine the first thing that happens is that our mind gets closer to our soul. The ambiance of the place helps us to get rid of our negativities.

Our thoughts become purer and all negative things like ego, jealousy, and greed go out of our mind. That's why when we visit such places people of all castes, creed, rich and poor move and pray together. Nobody thinks that he is rich or superior. They all have common thoughts and faith. When we bow our head and seek His blessings we discard our ego.

Large numbers of devotees carry out voluntary manual jobs in temples. Such actions help them in overcoming their negative propensities and make them better human beings by bringing their mind and soul together through the actions of their body. Thus it helps them to integrate Body Mind and Soul, and result is the ideal state of inner happiness.

Even our Courts make use of this activity by ordering petty criminals, particularly youngsters, to carry out manual jobs at religious places as part of the punishment. The idea is make the accused, particularly if he is a youngster, realize that he has committed a crime and his negative propensities need to be removed/ reduced. Penance is very effective way to achieve this.

If this spirit is missing or there is lack of faith, then no amount of prayer or visits will have any effect. At the end of the day, it is we who feel better and de-stressed after such visits because we have overcome the evils of ego, greed and jealousy, to some extent.

During such visits we also break away from our external environment and spend some time with ourselves, thereby reflecting on our actions, both, positive and negative. Our visit does not affect the Deity we visit. We are not doing any favors to the Deity. Such visits only benefit us.

We land in trouble because of our negative actions. Normally we don't accept the fact that we have erred. We rationalize our actions. These actions could be guided by greed or ego or jealousy. We ignore our inner voice and therefore lose track of the right path.

Prayers and visits to temples and religious places put us back on the right path and thus help us in overcoming our problems. They help us in cleansing our mind and thus overcome our negativities.

There is another dimension of faith and how it helps us. In times of stress one tends to feel dejected and helpless. If something is not done then there is every possibility that the individual may 'surrender' to circumstances. He may feel that this is his fate. He may go in depression. This means that he will stop facing the problem. If this happens, it will be a very big setback for him. Under such circumstances faith provides the much required ray of hope. It sends positive vibes to the mind. Mind in turn provides strength and courage to the individual to face the crises fairly and squarely. Finally individual comes out of the problem. This has double effect on the individual. Firstly that he has overcome the crisis and secondly he has come out a victorious person. The second aspect also enriches one's personality.

The hard fact we must realize is that there are no shortcut for solving our problems and only we have to find solutions to our problems.

Faith gives us,
Wisdom to know the
right from wrong,
An anchor in raging sea,
Calm in mist of chaos,
and courage to express it.

—*Anonymous*

Faith only provides us a way out and strengthen our mind to fight out our problem.

Under ideal conditions, our actions (Mind) should be in tune with the wishes of our soul. All our efforts and thinking should be guided by this, to achieve true happiness and peace of mind. Spirituality is the way to achieve this goal.

Power of Healing

Our body has all the power to heal itself. It is our immune system which provides us this power of healing. Stronger our immune system is more resistant our body will be to diseases and in case we fall sick, quicker will our recovery be. Medicines assist the body to fight infections and strengthen our immune system..

If you accidentally get a cut on your finger, the cut heals

itself. We apply bandage only to prevent

infection of the wound. The healing quality of our body is so good that even the original finger prints get formed at the injured place, after complete healing. The faster the wound is healed healthier our body is. In case of diabetic patient it takes much longer for body to heal the wounds.

Blessings—Power of Blessings

When we bow our head and pay respect to our elders, guru and God, we get their blessings. Blessings are one of the purest responses that we get when we bow in front of our gurus, elders, seniors because blessings come right from the heart/soul of the giver. Blessings are pure and

unpolluted by machinations of
the mind of the giver.

Another peculiar thing about
blessings is that whenever
somebody bows in front of his
elders or guru, they have to
bless him. They have no choice.
It is mandatory. So even if
your enemy comes and seek your
blessings by bowing in front
of you, you will find yourself
blessing him automatically. This
happens almost involuntarily and
it comes from your soul.

The best thing about blessings
is that all of us have the power
to give blessings irrespective of
our age, sex, rich/ poor, caste
or religion.

In Mahabharata, Shri Krishana
plays a master stroke. Before
going to the battle field, Sri
Krishana takes Pandavas to King
Dhritrashtra and Gandhari to seek
their blessings, fully knowing
that the Pandavas are going at
war against their sons. Although,

Dhritrashtra and Kunti were their elders but still they were in a fix. How could they bless those who are going to fight against them. Still they had no choice but to bless the Pandvas. If blessings did not have the power, Lord Krisna would not have taken Pandvas to Dhritrashtra and Kunti. So, if you seek blessings from even your arch enemy he will have to bless you and blessings will be sincere because they come from his soul.

I realized the importance of blessings when I became General Manager of an organization in Mumbai way back in 1990. The employees of this organization were very good in dramatics. They used to participate in State level competitions. Once they had prepared a Play and had booked an auditorium for the same. I was invited as chief guest and I went there along with my family.

Before the beginning of the play, they took me and my wife to the green room and briefed us about the play, which was in Marathi. After that they started introducing all participants such as director, writer, musicians, actors etc. While they were doing this, everybody, including ladies and young girls started touching our feet. Since we are North Indian, where ladies and young girls touch feet of their in-laws only, after their marriage, we felt uncomfortable and therefore objected.

The Director of the play told me that this is their tradition. He also told us that to seek our blessings is their right and we should not deny them this right. It was there that I realized the importance of seeking blessings. Though it is sign of respect towards the blessing giver but it is the blessing seeker who gets the real benefit of blessings.

If one seeks blessings sincerely, the blessings do have their effect. The blessing recipient does get the benefit of blessings. Another peculiarity about blessings is that blessings give benefit to the recipient only and no benefit to the blessing giver. Since Blessings come from the soul of the blessing giver, they have full effect on the recipient.

Is Soul Indestructible

Yes, soul cannot be created nor destroyed. That is the thinking as on date. If that be so, then the number of souls should be fixed and remain constant. That means the number of living things is fixed. The soul moves from the body to another after death.

What happens when soul leaves one dead body but no new 'body' is available to enter? Under such circumstances the soul wanders till it finds a new body. In real life we have seen it happen.

During wars or natural calamities when all of a sudden very large number of people die and large number of souls get released, it is not possible to have equal number of new bodies available to accommodate these souls, immediately. Therefore, large numbers of souls continue to wander till they find suitable bodies. Such places are therefore called Ghost Towns. That's why whenever someone dies, we always pray that the soul may rest in peace and may not have to wander in search of new body.

Action Plan IV

➢ Whenever in doubt. listen to your inner voice. Don't ignore it or rationalize your actions.

➢ Don't harm anybody or curse anybody. If you do then you will have to carry this dead weight throughout your life. With such actions you can never be at peace with yourself.

➢ Whenever you curse any person your soul cautions you against it. At such times you ignore your inner voice (soul) because you are guided by your negative propensities like jealousy, ego or greed. You may lie to the whole world but you know that you have done a wrong thing. Such actions will continue to haunt you. The only way left is either you say sorry to the person concerned and seek his forgiveness. Or you seek penance from Him .Till you do this you just can't have peace of mind.

➢ Get as many blessings as possible. Get blessings from your God, your Guru, your parents, relatives, elders. Don't hesitate; accumulate as much as you can. Only the fortunate ones get blessed or the blessed are fortunate.

➢ Get a guru, mentor or follow your religion with all sincerity. If you chose a living Guru, have full faith but don't have blind faith. As this world is full of fake Gurus who are out to exploit their gullible followers. To avoid this, it is better to have some saint, who has taken Samadhi, as Guru.

➢ There is no harm in attending discourses of learned people and having respect for them but be careful before you repose blind faith in them. As in such cases when there is breach of faith, it hurts the most. It hurts your mind far more than your body.

Great souls have wills,
feeble souls have only wishes.

—*Anonymous*

5. INTEGRATE—MIND + BODY + SOUL

To reach great heights, you must have great depths.

Integration of Soul, Mind and Body is the ultimate goal of spirituality. It is ultimate stage of achieving 'ONENESS'. When we integrate mind body and soul we achieve excellence, the ultimate bliss and sublime experience. That should be the aim of each one of us.

If all of us achieve this, then this world will be free from all the negative propensities like ego, greed and jealousy etc. Our earth will become heaven like. Yes, it is very difficult to achieve complete integration of Body, Mind and Soul but by moving in this direction we can achieve success varying between 60%—80%. Even this achievement will make this world a better place to live.

We must continue to develop our mind through formal/informal training and learn from others and our own experience. We must recognize our weak areas and try to overcome our weaknesses and negativities like ego, greed, anger, jealousy etc . Keep good company and enrich your mind through good thoughts and deeds.

Let us see how one can overcome these negative traits.

As a human being, it is very difficult to not have negative traits. It is very easy to suggest that we should overcome our negativities. Ask those who have developed habit of drinking and smoking. Knowing fully their adverse affect on their health and wellbeing, they still find it very difficult to overcome these habits. It is easier said than done. We pick up such negative traits through our immediate social environment and through our experience.

But there is a way out. For overcoming any bad habit or negative trait, the best way is to replace it with a positive habit or trait. For achieving this one needs determination. We can adopt the following road map.

Replace Ego with Self-Esteem & Humility

Ego and self-esteem are just like two sides of the same coin. Whereas ego is a negative trait, self-esteem is not only a positive trait but a very healthy and essential trait. In the long run ego is a self-destructive trait. It encourages selfishness, false pride and self-righteousness. It makes the person blind to logic and balanced thinking. He looks down upon others and treats them with contempt.

Self-esteem on the other hand, pushes you towards worthy goals and success, there by leading to happiness, in the long run. It helps in having faith in yourself, a prerequisite for achieving anything worthwhile.

Having faith in oneself also helps in facing problems and sailing through tough times. One of the best ways to improve your self-esteem is by way of doing social service. Help the poor and needy. Give more than you get.

Develop the habit of giving more than you get, without any ulterior motive. Give a little more than you can afford. May it be in cash or kind or even intangible like love, affection, a complement or a praise. Practice 'Art of Giving'.

One doesn't have to be great,
being human is itself an achievement

—*Anonymous*

Replace Greed with Ambition

Greed is when one desires for things far beyond his requirements and the urge to get more, without putting in any efforts. To adopt unfair means to accumulate materialistic things. Through greed you may be able to achieve material success in the short term but it will not give you peace of mind. Your mind will always be in state of turbulence. This happens because once you are successful in fulfilling your greed, your mind propels you to go further thereby increasing your greed.

In this way you enter a vicious circle which has no end. You have unknowingly taken a path which leads only to frustration and unhappiness, in the long run.

Ambition on the other hand is a positive trait. It can actually be the driving force to achieve your goals and fulfill your dreams. To achieve ones ambition one has to work hard with commitment and through fair means. Then and only then you experience happiness and taste true success. By replacing greed with ambition one gets multidimensional pleasure of success, achievement and lasting contentment.

Replace Jealousy with Self Confidence

Jealousy is a negative trait. The worst part is that, jealousy is always towards people who are close to you. One would only be jealous of his friends, relatives or neighbors.

It is strange but true that you are never jealous of people whom you don't know. Just imagine the implications. Shouldn't we be loving people around us instead of being jealous?

Jealousy is such a dangerous trait that it makes one hate those people whom he should be actually loving.

What are the causes of jealousy?

It could be due to inferiority complex or due to your incompetence or it could be just your attitude. Some people just can't stand when someone is successful or happy. Jealousy does nothing positive. It only upsets your mind and causes tension. Through jealousy you can't achieve anything. It only harms you by causing stress and related problems. It ruins your relationships. Imagine, jealousy does not affect the person you are jealous of. It is such a bad trait but still one of the most common traits.

Strangely, there are only two people who will never be jealous of you, your mother and your guru.

Self-confidence on the other hand is a positive trait. It gives birth to new desires. You yearn to get what the other person has got. You start working towards new goals. It makes you work hard towards your goals. Self-confidence leads to progress.

Replace Revenge with Forgiveness

When we feel hurt or cheated the urge to take revenge is born. This urge is spontaneous. Our ego is hurt. Either we react immediately or start planning the ways to take revenge. Since at that particular time our mind is in disturbed/agitated state, whatever we do is likely to have serious consequences. Under such circumstances we are likely to commit not mistakes but blunders which we will regret afterwards. But the damage has been done and our mind remains disturbed and this leads to stress.

When we plan for taking revenge our mind becomes agitated. Though our Soul (mentor) advises us against it but still we rationalize and seek revenge. Revenge has another dimension. When we take revenge we enter a vicious circle. When we take revenge, the affected person will also react and may take revenge. This leads to nothing but stress and thereby affecting your health. When you take this path you can never be at peace. The resultant stress will adversely affect your wellbeing and performance.

To love means loving the unlovable
To forgive means pardon
the unpardonable
Faith means believing
the unbelievable
Hope means hoping when
Everything looks hopeless

G. Chesterton

The best option under such circumstances is to forgive your adversary for whatever wrong he has done. Forgiveness is divine. It is one of the most difficult things to do. One has to suppress one's ego. But when we forgive, it brings about a feeling of serenity, a strange sense of bliss. It is a great stress reliever.

Super Natural Powers

Any ability of a living being which can't be explained through logic is super natural power. Knowingly or unknowingly we all have some super natural power or we are capable of having super natural powers. We may have some super natural power but may not be aware of it. For example Hanuman ji didn't know that he had the power to fly and therefore he never attempted to fly. It was during war with Ravan that he was told that he had the power to fly. Similarly Angad did not know that if he touched any stone, it will not sink in water but will remain afloat. Or maybe he had knowledge as to what kind of stone sinks in water and what type of stone floats on water. Today we all know that Pumice stone floats on water. He exercised this super natural power only after he became aware of it.

In our case, for example each one of us has the power of, what is known as the third eye and all of make use of this to a small extent, unknowingly. To prove this, just conduct this experiment:

Keep some 8 to 10 coins of 50 paisa, one and two rupee denomination in your back pocket. Now try to take out one Re.1 coin. You will observe that while trying to locate the one rupee coin you will concentrate on your pocket, which you can't see, and to increase your concentration, unknowingly, you will close your eyes. Logically, when you are looking for something your eyes should be wide open but in this case you do the opposite and close your eyes. In reality what you are doing is that you are trying to use your 3rd. eye and to enable it to look for the desired coin. You don't want any distractions, so you close your eyes.

Some people will say that by closing our eyes we are trying to concentrate. Very true, concentration is the first step towards the power of third eye. While conducting this experiment, you will notice that your mind will be trying to have a look inside your pocket. If you concentrate more you can really have a look through your third eye.

Our body and mind are so powerful that each one of us can have super natural powers. All that is needed is strong belief in yourself, concentration and abhyasa. If we want, we can look into our past and future as well. But this requires determination and abhyasa. We have to get rid of our petty thinking and negativities to achieve any super natural power.

We have read in scriptures that the Devtas had the capability of reaching any place, instantaneously. This is nothing but teleporting. Today research is going on and the day is not far when we will have this capability.

Miracles

What are miracles? Miracles are those events which defy any logic and rational explanation. We come across a number of miracles in our day to day life. Unfortunately, most of the miracles are performed by so called fake godmen or spiritual gurus. Most of these miracles are either fake or tricks played on gullible audience.

According to such godmen, these so called miracles are considered necessary to develop/ imbibe faith in the followers. To some extent it is true because it is faith which is essential for achieving any worthwhile results. Without inculcating faith in followers no godman or spiritual guru can produce any results.

However it will be wrong to treat all miracles as fake or tricks. Some of the miracles are genuine but such genuine miracles are rare and far between. The fact that we are unable to explain such events is due to lack of ability/ understanding on our part. If we look around, miracles have been attributed to almost all saints and godmen. Some of such events were miracles. Some of the events got exaggerated over a period of time. In some cases, today such miracles may appear logical but when they were performed, people considered them as miracles. This happens more out of ignorance than anything else. In Christianity, sainthood is awarded by the Pope only after it is proved that a particular individual has performed some miracle. Mother Teresa has been honored with sainthood based on verifiable miracles performed by her.

Therefore miracles are part and parcel of spirituality but we should be careful and fall in traps laid by fake gurus.

Achieving Starts from Believing

*—**Anonymous***

Action Plan V

- ➢ Yoga is the best way to integrate Mind, Body and Soul. It helps calm the mind, provides exercise to the whole body including all the organs and brings mind and soul closer.
- ➢ Replace Ego with Self-Esteem
- ➢ Replace Jealousy with Self Confidence
- ➢ Replace Desires with Goals
- ➢ Replace Greed with Ambition/ achievement motivation
- ➢ Don't try to change the world. Change yourself and become a good human being.
- ➢ Give more than you get.

6. THE REALITY CHECK

We should not ignore or justify our negativities. These negativities make a person 'Bundle of Blunders'. Because of these negative propensities, all of us, at some stage of life commit mistakes. These mistakes, over a period of time get converted to blunders but then it is too late to take corrective actions,

You will find many families and big business houses which have gone down the drain because of greed of the main stake holders. Lot of enterprises and families lost fortune because of ego and lethargy of their key persons. They expected others to work and earn for them.

Even lust has been cause of downfall of many individuals and families. Our negativities ruin us slowly, without our realizing it. By the time we realize, it is normally too late. The process becomes almost irreversible. The only way out is that the concerned individuals accept their mistakes and take the path of spirituality.

Then, there are those people who, all their life blame anybody and everybody for their failures. Such people never accept their mistakes. When they fail they never accept responsibility of their actions. These are signs of a weak personality. Because they never accept their mistakes, they never improve. In the process they continue to suffer. In some cases this attitude and habit even passes on to the next generation and their downfall starts even before they take-off in life.

To succeed on life, one must accept responsibility for his actions, both good and bad. One should not pass on responsibility and use others as whipping boys, for one's own mistakes.

Story of a Noble Man

Here is a story to show who is a true noble man.

I was heading an organization of almost 3000 employees in Mumbai. One day a union leader of a nearby organization came to see me. He told me that he was looking for one government letter and if it was available in my office, he wanted a copy of the letter.

Being a union leader of another organization, I could not be rude to him but I also did not want him to interact with my staff, directly. So I called the concerned person and told him to get the letter. Since it was an old letter, the whole action had to take time. With union leader sitting in front of me, I also could not do my normal work.

To pass time, I started asking him about his job environment and finally I asked him about his family. He told me that he has four children. The eldest son was married and was working in Dubai, his one daughter was married and settled in Kolhapur, another daughter was in 6th standard and the youngest daughter was in 4th standard. I was surprised at the age gap between children. Sensing my surprise, he explained that the eldest two are his children. The younger two girls were children of one of the employees who died in an accident.

Although the wife of that employee got a government job but

she was not in a position to look after the two daughters so he had adopted them. He told me with sense of pride that he will ensure that they get good education before he finally gets them married. He made these statements in such a **matter of fact** manner, which was surprising.

All of a sudden, looking at him, while sitting in the General Manager's chair, I felt very small in front of him. Here was a person who is spiritually, really great and he is doing wonders, silently. HE IS GIVING MUCH MORE THAN HE IS GETTING. That's the 'Art of Giving'.

In real life however, one comes across situations which are not only frustrating but outright disgusting. Many of us have helped our friends and relatives, financially and materially at the time of their need.. But sometimes the person you have helped, thinks that you

are nave and he is smart. Instead
of appreciating your good deeds,
they think they have fooled you
through their sweet talk. Such
experiences should not deter you
from the path of giving

Art of living Lies in Art of giving.

—*B.S. Ahluwalia*

Pseudo Spirituality

Pseudo spirituality is practiced by fake gurus. These are the persons who have brought spirituality a bad name. The world is full of such pseudo gurus whose main objective is to fool and fleece innocent public, in the name of religion. Then there are those who preach violence in the name of religion although no religion preaches violence.

Faith is a very powerful force because for faith, people are even prepared to die. Such gurus exploit this power of faith which their followers have in them. Then there are such dharma gurus who start off well but as they become powerful and rich, they get drifted towards materialism. Instead of being gurus they end up as businessmen by commercializing spirituality. They become so greedy that they start adopting unfair means to achieve their corrupted commercial objectives.

The other type of dharma gurus/leaders are those who preach violence in the name of spirituality/religion. There is no place for violence in spirituality. No religion preaches violence. Such gurus misinterpret religion for their personal gains. Such gurus are very egoistic and are hungry for power. Their agenda is to become powerful and they use spirituality/religion to achieve their goals, at the cost of their gullible followers.

It is such pseudo gurus which are discouraging people from taking the spiritual path. In reality, in our heart of heart most of us want to be spiritual because it brings about total development of the individual. But instances of fake gurus and greedy spiritual leaders put them off.

Faith is to believe what
you do not yet see,
The reward for this faith is
to see what you believe.

—*St. Augustine*

Synopsis

Nature has given us the wonderful machine called body. Our body has enormous potential and capabilities. On an average we use only 25 to 30 % of our capabilities.

If through spirituality we increase our body usage by even 10%, we will not only be healthy but one of the prosperous people.

Practice self-discipline. Yes, discipline is very essential, whether it is your food habits, doing physical exercise, life style or nurturing relationships. Discipline is the bottom line to achieve anything worthwhile.

To exploit fuller potential and to enjoy the fruits of our success, we need to have a healthy body and a calm Mind. Spirituality provides total solution to achieve this, through pranayama, yoga and meditation. We don't need to spend long hours to achieve this, even a few minutes are enough we do such things sincerely and regularly.

The other thing required to achieve this is to have a healthy life style and food habits. We must be careful about what we eat because that has direct bearing on our health and mind. For this it is necessary that we take fresh Satvik food. By healthy life style we mean active live which should include some physical exercise and avoids laid back attitude. If you have time, develop some hobby which gives you satisfaction and a sense of achievement.

The second most important part of our being is the Mind—though invisible but most critical part. All our good and bad deeds are done at the command of our mind. All your thoughts and actions are controlled by your mind. To lead healthy and successful life one needs to;

Enriched your mind through education, experience and training.

- Have purity of thoughts and deeds through spirituality.
- Have company of people of character and integrity.
- Avoid and overcome negative habits by replacing them with positive habits.
- Have high integrity and avoid short cuts to achieve success.
- Avoid negativities like greed, lust, jealousy, anger and ego.
- Have high self-esteem by giving more than you get.
- Keep your knowledge and skills updated through training and continuous learning.
- Dream big and work towards achieving/fulfilling them.

- Develop art of listening. Keep your mind open for views of others and new ideas.

As we go through our life, there are occasions when we have to take some important decisions. It becomes difficult to choose between the various options available to us.

Under these circumstances it is best to put the various options to, what is known as 'Rotary Test'. The test is to evaluate the various options as under:

- Is it the truth?
- Is it fair to all concerned?
- Will it build goodwill and better relationships?
- Will it be beneficial to all concerned?

Whichever option passes this test is the best under the circumstances.

Action Plan VI

➢ Write down your Mission Statement and also what you want to become in life.

➢ Prepare a five year road map of your goals and targets.

➢ Put these in your computer as home page or screen saver so that you automatically view them regularly.

➢ Review your road map every year to ascertain your success rate.

➢ Analyze reasons for shortfalls.

➢ Don't blame others or rationalize your failures.

➢ You are responsible for both, success and failure.

➢ If you have erred accept it.

➢ Modify your next five year plan according to changed

circumstances and your experiences.

- ➢ If you feel stressed, find reasons for this. Stress is bad for health and has direct bearing on your performance. It is self-defeating.
- ➢ Think ways and means of reducing stress.
- ➢ If required modify your plan. Other option could be, develop some hobby.
- ➢ Do something which you enjoy. If required, seek help of a Mentor.
- ➢ Make it a habit, before going to bed, relax for five minutes and dispassionately review your day's activities.
- ➢ What positive and negative things you have done. Did you give complement to any person?
- ➢ Any achievements or mistakes? If you have hurt anybody, take immediate corrective action by saying sorry.

- ➢ Saying sorry, if you have erred or hurt any person, is a great quality and a great stress buster.
- ➢ Develop habit of giving genuine complements.
- ➢ This will help you to remain focused, otherwise, without realizing, over a period of time, you lose focus, get entangled in relationship problems and waste your time on petty and insignificant things.
- ➢ Remember one thing, no negative action or thought, however strong, will benefit you in the long run.
- ➢ Do yoga/exercise and pranayama on regular basis.
- ➢ The best way to do this is to join a group of likeminded people.
- ➢ This will encourage and motivate you to become regular in such activities.

Fragrance never leaves the hand
That gives flowers of joy.

—*Chinese Proverb*

SNIPPETS

1. In London Olympics, a legally blind South Korean player shoots 1st, world mark in archery. This is power of mind and the power of 3rd. eye.
2. AAT—Animal assisted therapy using dogs is being to cheer up children suffering from serious medical

problems. This therapy accelerates recovery.

3. 2nd Aug, 2012 news item: Asthma common among Olympic athletes. Asthma was the most common chronic conditions among athletes and could be related to intense training, according to study conducted by University of Western Australian, over last five Oly. Games. Inhaling polluted or cold air is also considered an important factor.

With all the physical exercise, actually the athletes should be in very good physical shape. Under such conditions the immunity of the body should be strong enough to protect against pollution etc.

In reality only the athletes who are competing in individual events are likely to suffer from Asthma because they are under great stress. Their countries have great expectations from them and winning the medal depends only on their performance. In case of team events the outcome is not individual based but whole team is responsible for the outcome.

So for in case of individual events the stakes are very high. It is therefore stress which is causing asthma, more than anything else.

4. Think you are fat you may grow fat. According to Norwegian

University of Science and Technology, it may be related to psychological stress, associated with gaining weight around the waist. YOU ARE WHAT YOUR THOUGHTS ARE.

5. According to Hay, a life coach, 'All diseases are the creation of our mind'. A well-controlled mind is the key to reduced stress and disease free life.

6. Heading in Times of India dt 21st. Oct. 2012—**'I beat cancer with willpower'**. Shri Sharad Pawar, cabinet minister, was diagnosed for cancer

soon after he had filed his papers for 2004 elections. Doctors had asked him to complete legal formalities like writing of Will etc. He was told that he would live for just another six months. The astute politician cheated death and emerged a winner. Shear willpower and inspiration from his mother helped him win the battle against the deadly cancer. Today he has fully recovered and does not need any treatment. THIS IS A GOOD EXAMPLE OF THE POWER OF OUR MIND AND CURING POWER OF OUR BODY .

7. Researchers at Oxford and Southampton University in UK have discovered that 87% doctors have used 'impure' placebo treatments, while 12% have used 'pure' placebos. A random sample of doctors found to be representative of all UK doctors registered with General Medical Council was surveyed on line with 78 responses. The results showed ethical attitudes and variation towards placebo usage among doctors. Around 84% of doctors said that impure placebos or

subjecting patients to unnecessary blood tests, X-Rays, or other body examinations were acceptable. Another 66% said that it was clinically acceptable to prescribe drugs without active ingredients, meaning they wouldn't work at all.

Why are some people rich and successful?

How did they achieve success?

Did they have an external influence or through their own hard work?

We all have desires and aspirations for money, power, and fame. At the back of it is the need for financial security and achievement. Although these things are common across people but there is huge variation as to what different people achieve in life. What are the reasons for this anomaly?

The reasons lie within us. Although there is no restriction in having dreams and wishes, we set very low targets and goals for ourselves. The hard fact is that you may achieve 70% or 90% of your target but you will never achieve more than your target. By setting lower target and by having lower aspirations you are only stunting your growth. To start with, all of us have same potential but most of us are not even aware of the powers of our Mind and our Body.

Prof. Ahluwalia highlights all these aspects and lays down the road map for you to realize your power and potential and how to succeed in life, achieving the success you richly deserve.

http://inspiredlifethebook.blogspot.in